IONA — DURHAM — FOUNTAINS ABBEY

SALISBURY — YORK

WESTMINSTER ABBEY — ST GEORGE'S CHAPEL

'S COLLEGE CHAPEL — ST PAUL'S — WESLEY'S CHAPEL

WESTMINSTER CATHEDRAL — COVENTRY — LIVERPOOL RC CATHEDRAL

Edinburgh Castle viewed from the city

GREAT BRITISH CASTLES

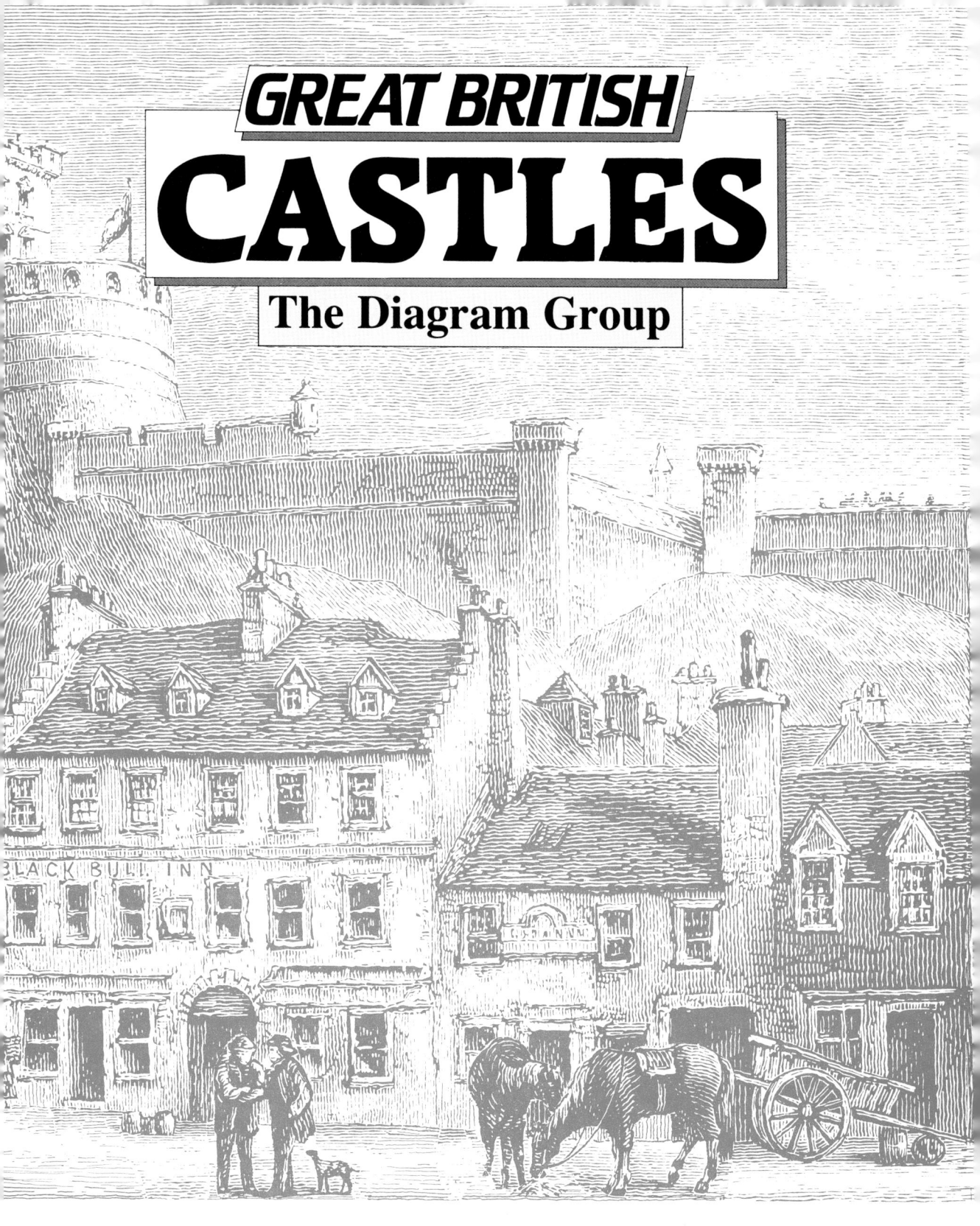

The Diagram Group

Franklin Watts
London New York Sydney Toronto

Acknowledgements
Picture Research: Patricia Robertson
Cover: The National Trust
Title page: Mansell Collection
British Library 21 (left)
CADW 25
Country Life 13
Hever Castle 33
Mansell Collection 10, 14, 15, 22-23, 29, 35
Popperfoto 21 (right)
Society of Antiquaries 6, 7
Studio St Ives Ltd 17

Contents

The parts of a castle	4
Maiden Castle	6
Tower of London	8
Arundel Castle	10
Dover Castle	12
Windsor Castle	14
Tintagel Castle	16
Leeds Castle	18
Caernarvon Castle	20
Conway Castle	22
Beaumaris Castle	24
Edinburgh Castle	26
Bodiam Castle	28
Warwick Castle	30
Hever Castle	32
Balmoral Castle	34
Castles of interest	36
Things to look for in a castle	38
Useful addresses	40
Index	41

© Diagram Visual Information Ltd 1987

First published in Great Britain 1987 by
Franklin Watts Ltd
12a Golden Square
London W1R 4BA

Printed in France

ISBN 0 86313 454 8

⁴ The parts of a castle

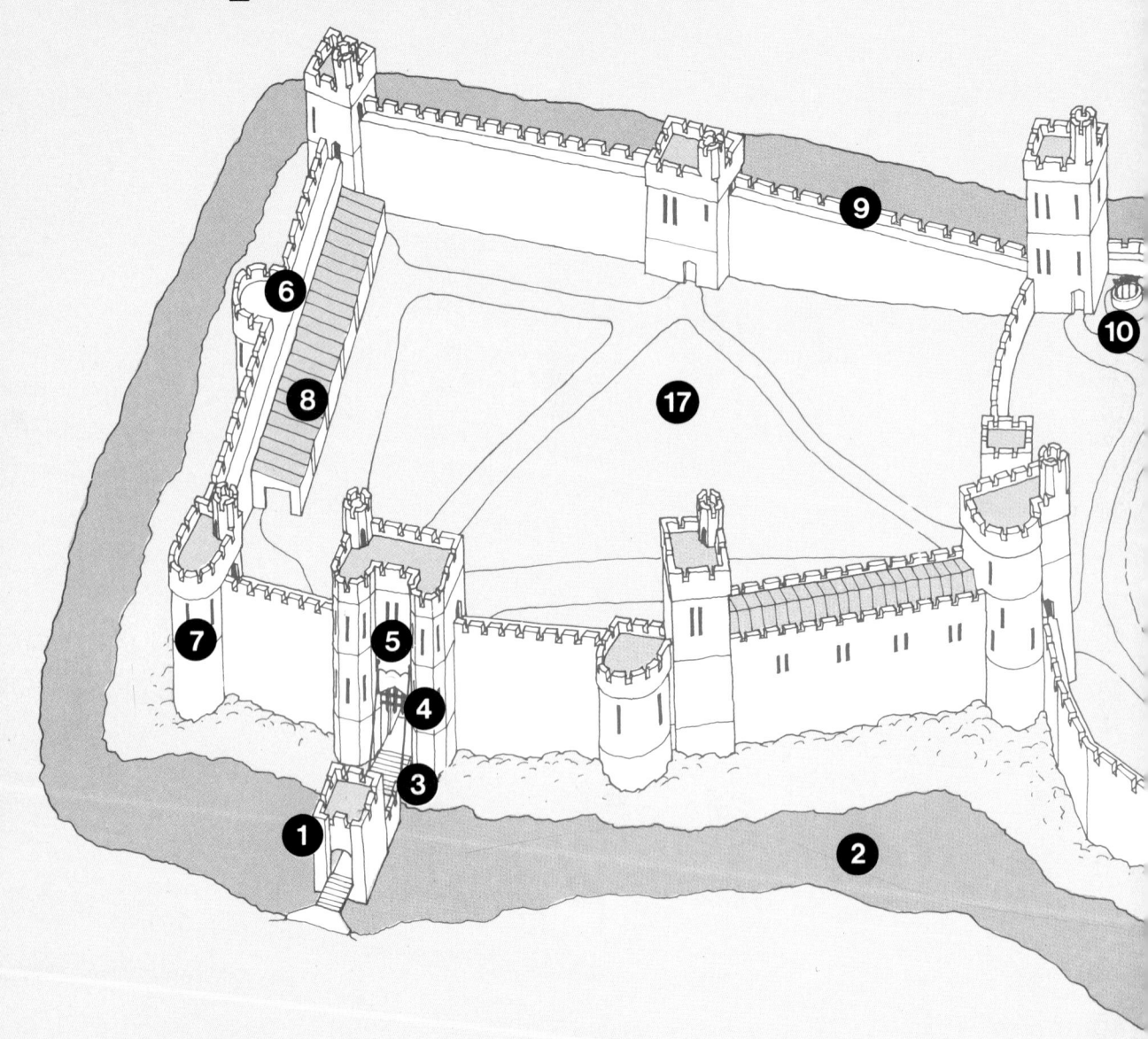

1. Barbican (outer defence)
2. Moat
3. Drawbridge
4. Portcullis
5. Gatehouse
6. Wall walk
7. Corner tower
8. Stables
9. Battlements
10. Well
11. Keep
12. Chapel
13. Motte (mound)
14. Household apartments
15. Great Hall
16. Kitchen and pantry
17. Bailey
18. Turret
19. Buttress
20. Curtain wall

5

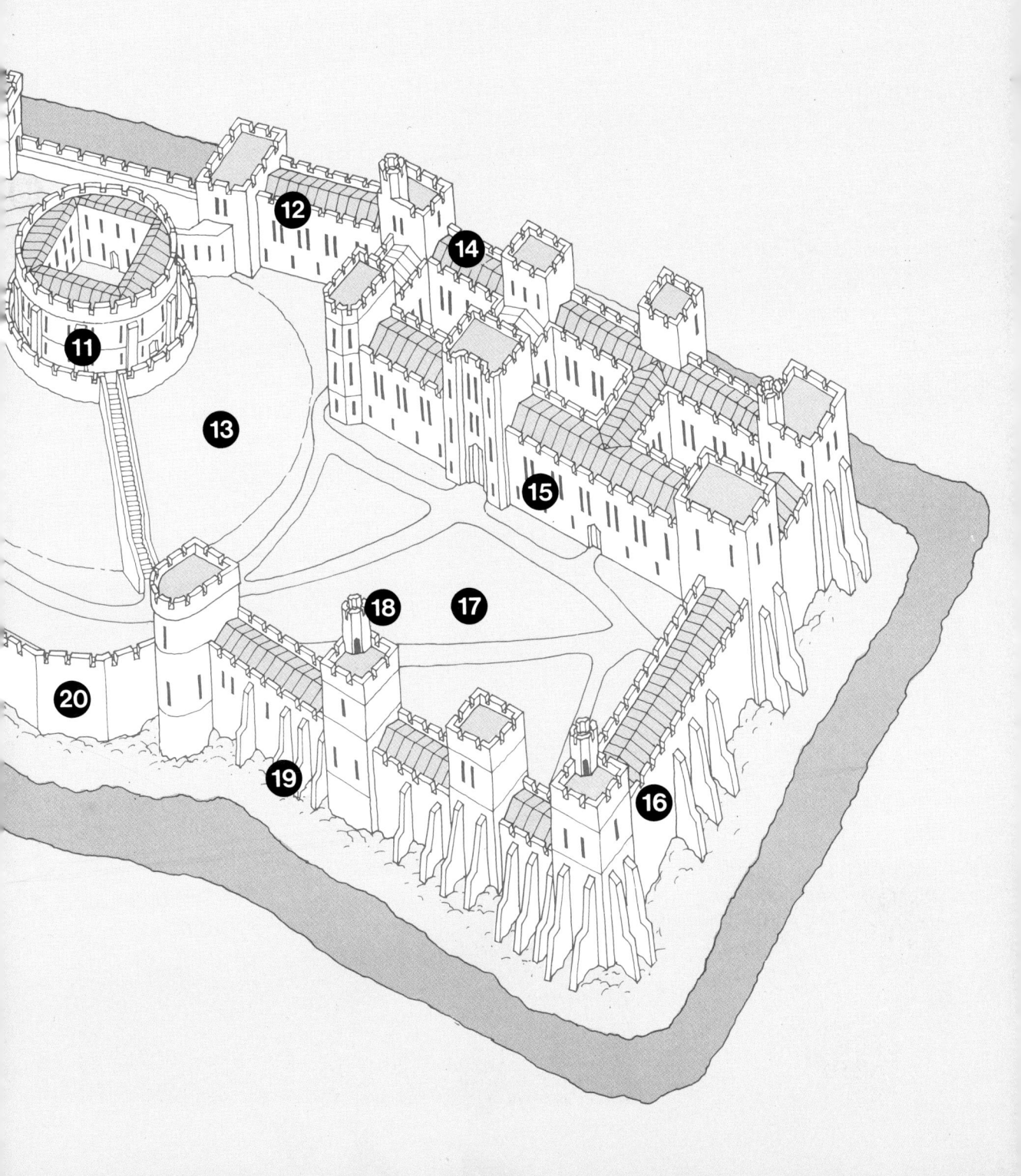

Maiden Castle

c 3000 BC
First Stone Age settlement on eastern side of hill
c 2000 BC
Funeral monument 537m (587yds) long dug on hilltop. Evidence of new settlers from Continent
c 1500 BC
Site deserted
c 300 BC
Maiden Castle built by European Iron Age settlers
c 75 BC
Extended defences included many banks and ditches
c AD 43
Roman legions break through fortifications
AD 70
Maiden Castle deserted
c 380
Roman temple built
Late 500s
Man buried on hilltop
1934-37
Sir Mortimer Wheeler directed excavations of Maiden Castle

The first inhabitants of Maiden Castle were late Stone Age people. They carved out their village on the eastern side of the high, flat hilltop in the Dorset countryside. For 1500 years, they lived peacefully within the 15 acres of ground protected by encircling ditches. They grew their crops, grazed their animals and made simple tools of bone and horn. Then the climate became harsher and the people left their homes.

A thousand years passed before new settlers came. Soon an Iron Age town sprawled over the 45 acres enclosed by a new stone wall. Houses were built and streets paved, cloth woven and food grown. Immigrants continued to arrive. They included refugees from Brittany fleeing from the advancing armies of Julius Caesar. These people built the system of ramparts (a maze of ditches and earth banks) as protection against invaders.

1 A general view from the west. The temple ruins and priest's house can be seen on the top left.

2 The backbone of a defender, killed by a Roman in AD 43. The arrowhead can be seen in the middle. It is on display at the Dorchester Museum.

3 Beach pebble slingstones were used as ammunition in the 1st century BC. Hoards of them were found. One pile had over 20,000 pebbles.

The complex of defences, however, was useless against the Roman armies. In AD 43-4, a legion, led by the future Emperor Vespasian, stormed the fortress and sacked the town. The surviving inhabitants left their ruined streets and houses and moved to the new Roman town of Dorchester.

Maiden Castle remained deserted until about AD 380, when a Roman temple was built, and a two-roomed house for the priest who tended it. Two hundred years later, one man was buried close to the now-ruined temple. All signs of habitation were slowly covered by soil and grass. The story of Maiden Castle was revealed by archaeologists in the 20th century. Relics and models can be seen in the museum in Dorchester. The origin of the name, however, is still a mystery.

A Stone Age man would have dressed like this in skins and carried simple tools.

3

Tower of London

William the Conqueror first built a fortress on the River Thames to defend the city of London. The only part of this fortress left is a large keep. It was finished after his death in 1087. Henry III had the keep whitewashed and it became known as the White Tower. He also had the outer walls built and extended the royal apartments in the inner ward. The Tower was used as a palace, a prison and an arms store. The royal zoo was started there in the 13th century when Henry III was given an elephant. For a time it also housed the Royal Mint and Treasury. It still guards the Crown Jewels.

The Tower of London is really a series of towers, with a moat, now dry. The inner ward is defended by a wall with thirteen towers and the outer ward by another wall with two bastions (half open towers) and six towers on the river side. The most famous tower is the Bloody Tower, believed to be called that after the suicide, in 1585, of Henry Percy, 8th Earl of Northumberland. This was also where the young princes, Edward V and the Duke of York, were murdered in 1483, and Sir Walter Ralegh imprisoned. The Tower was the scene of murders, executions and solitary confinements. Many prisoners passed through

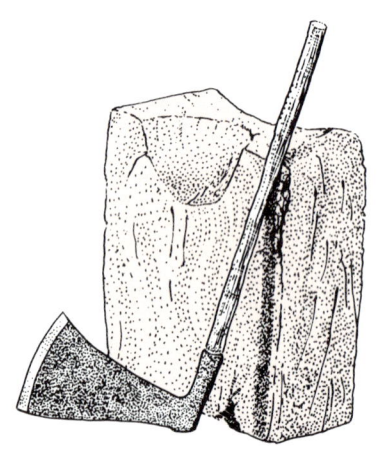

The execution block and axe were last used in England in 1747 when Lord Lovat was beheaded for treason.

c 1078
First Norman keep built
1241
Keep whitewashed
1471
Henry VI died in Wakefield Tower
1509
Yeoman Warders founded
c 1530
The Queen's House built
1536
Anne Boleyn beheaded
1542
Catherine Howard beheaded
1603
Sir Walter Ralegh imprisoned
1671
Attempted theft of Crown Jewels
1834
Zoo moved to Regent's Park
1941
Rudolf Hess, Hitler's deputy, kept in Tower
1974
Terrorist bomb exploded in White Tower. One dead, 37 injured

The Imperial State Crown. This was made in 1838 for the coronation of Queen Victoria and contains over 3,000 precious stones. The Crown Jewels are on display.

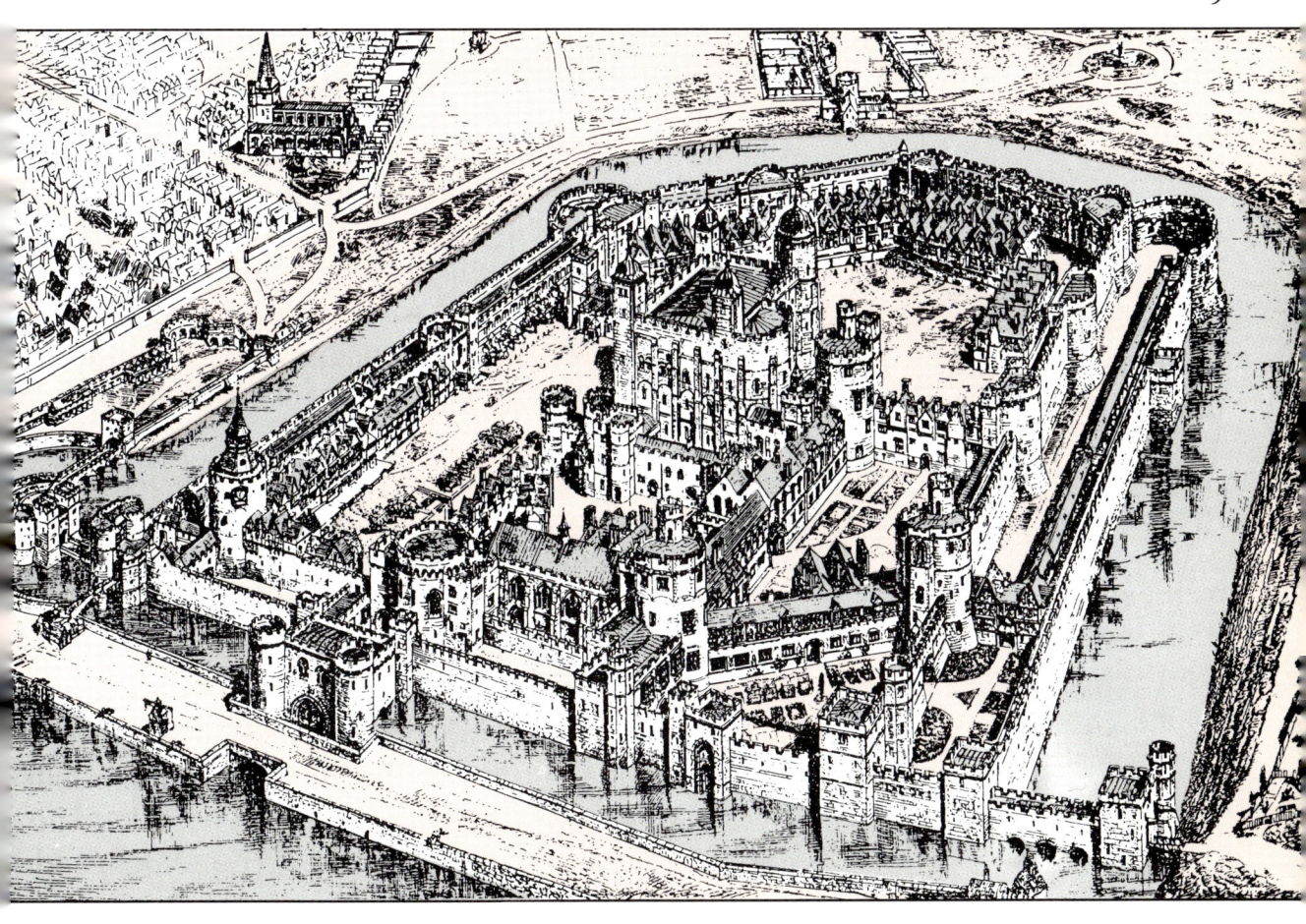

Traitor's Gate to St Thomas' Tower and the scaffold. Among them were Thomas More, Henry VIII's minister, and two of Henry VIII's wives, Anne Boleyn and Catherine Howard.

The Tower Armouries is the oldest museum in England. It contains many examples of arms and armour, including some made for Henry VIII and his horse. By tradition, Yeoman Warders, in their bright red uniforms, guard the Tower and royal salutes are fired from the guns on the wharf. For the sovereign's birthday, accession or coronation, or a great State event, 62 guns are fired, and 41 for the opening of parliament or birth of a royal child.

A reconstruction of the Tower as it would have looked in the 16th century. Traitor's Gate is at the front towards the left, by the river.

The ravens are looked after by the Yeoman Ravenmaster. Legend has it that if the ravens leave the Tower, the British Empire and the White Tower will collapse.

Arundel Castle

The Fitzalan-Howard Coat of Arms which dates back to 1556 when the two families were united by marriage.

The first castle was built on a chalk hill overlooking the River Arun in Sussex in 1067 by Roger de Montgomery, Earl of Arundel. He was given the land by William the Conqueror as a reward for maintaining order in Normandy while William was conquering England. The original timber fortifications were replaced by a stone shell keep in 1138. This still exists today.

The layout of the castle is similar to Windsor. Both have a motte (mound) on which the keep stands. There is an upper and lower bailey (courtyard) surrounded by a curtain wall with a gatehouse set in it. In 1243, the castle was inherited by the Fitzalan family. They held it, except for brief periods when it was seized by the Crown, until 1556. Then Thomas Howard, the 4th Duke of Norfolk, married Mary Fitzalan, and the Dukes of Norfolk have held the castle ever since.

The castle was badly damaged in the Civil War in 1643. Marks of the cannon fire can still be seen on the walls above the barbican (outer defence) archway. Oliver Cromwell's men occupied Arundel for five years (1644-49) and wrecked the interior. The castle remained in ruins until the 18th century, when various repairs were done by the 8th and 11th Dukes of Norfolk. The 15th

A view of the Norman battlements which were reconstructed and completed in 1903.

Duke of Norfolk finally completed the restoration and reconstruction from 1875 to 1903.

There are many treasures in the castle. These include robes, costumes, paintings, arms and armour, a late 16th-century German backgammon board, the prayer book and gold rosary carried by Mary Queen of Scots at her execution. The library is 37m (122ft) long and contains 10,000 books. A banner flies from the Well Tower in the keep when the present Duke of Norfolk, the 17th, is in residence.

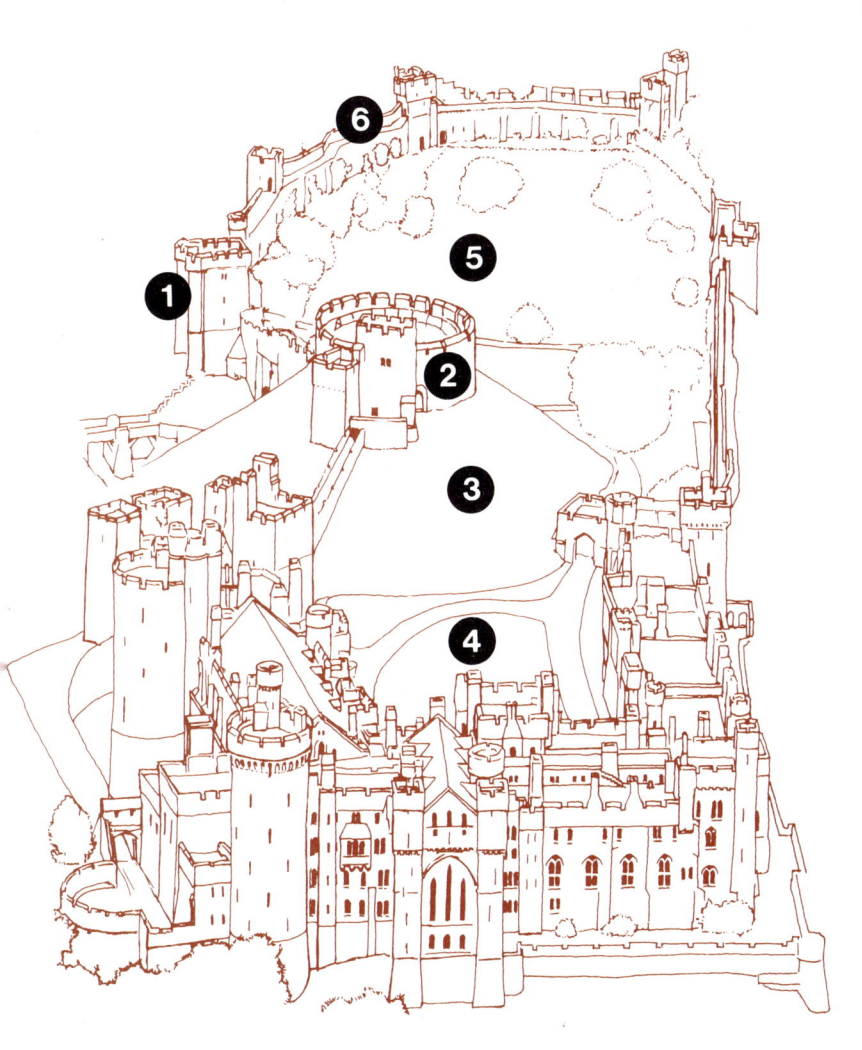

1067
First motte and bailey castle built
1138
Stone shell keep built
1295
Gatehouse built with portcullis, drawbridge and two towers
1380
Fitzalan Chapel built
1643
Castle besieged and sacked by Parliamentarians
1787
Restoration work began
1846
Queen Victoria visited castle
1903
Reconstruction completed

An aerial drawing of Arundel Castle showing:
1 The barbican
2 The Well Tower and keep
3 The motte (mound)
4 The quadrangle (lower bailey)
5 Tilting Yard (upper bailey, now private)
6 The curtain wall

Dover Castle

Dover Castle in Kent stands on a cliff top. It overlooks the shortest route between Britain and France, and has been of strategic importance throughout English history.

Earthworks show that it was once an Iron Age hill fort. The Romans used it later and built the lighthouse you can still see today. The Normans built a timber motte and bailey castle after their conquest of Britain in 1066. The stone castle was begun in the reign of Henry II (1154-89). The cube-shaped keep has walls which are so thick that they contain tiny rooms. The keep is surrounded by an inner wall with fourteen towers, two gatehouses and two barbicans. The outer curtain wall was also started then. This shows that Dover is the first castle known in western Europe to have used concentric fortification (one within the other). King John extended the royal apartments and the outer curtain wall. It has many towers and forms a U-shape round the castle. The open edge runs along the top of the cliffs.

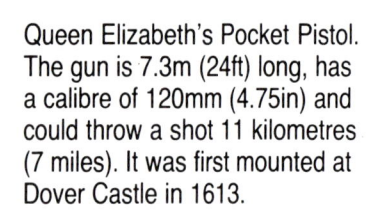

The south east coast of England showing the Cinque Ports: 1 Sandwich, 2 Dover, 3 Hythe, 4 Romney and 5 Hastings. From late Anglo-Saxon times until 1685 they provided ships for the king's service.

Queen Elizabeth's Pocket Pistol. The gun is 7.3m (24ft) long, has a calibre of 120mm (4.75in) and could throw a shot 11 kilometres (7 miles). It was first mounted at Dover Castle in 1613.

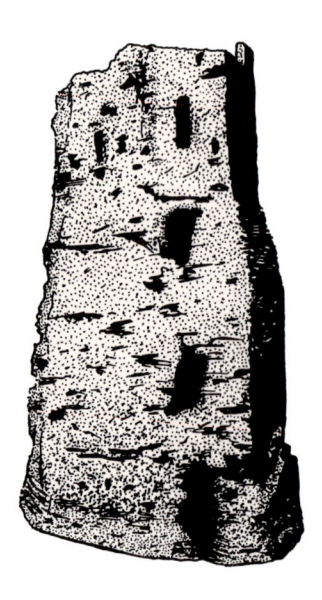

One of the two Roman lighthouses. It was rebuilt in the 15th century but was about 24m (80ft) high.

An aerial view of Dover Castle. The Constable's Gate is at the middle front of the picture.

In 1216, the French besieged the castle and badly damaged the North Gate. Henry III built a new entrance, the Constable's Gate, finished in 1227. It was a massive structure and was the residence of the constable (governor of the castle). Now the deputy lives there. The present constable is Her Majesty Queen Elizabeth the Queen Mother. Previous ones included Sir Winston Churchill.

The castle was mostly completed by about 1250 and survived for 500 years. In the 18th century, it was altered. Many of the towers on the outer wall were cut down to mount cannons and provide for artillery. Defensive earthworks were dug because earth absorbed the shock of cannon fire better than stone. In spite of these changes, Dover Castle is still very impressive and has retained its medieval character.

1066
Normans built timber castle
1154
Stone castle started by Henry II
1205
Royal apartments and defences improved by King John
1216
French attacked castle
1250
Castle mostly completed
1642
Castle held by Parliamentarians in Civil War
1745
Alterations begun
1803
Earthworks dug for cannons
1958
Garrison withdrawn'
1961-63
Archaeological dig revealed evidence of Norman bank and ditch
1963
Castle given to Ministry of Public Building and Works

Windsor Castle

Windsor Castle in Berkshire is the largest inhabited castle in the world. It is also the oldest of the three official royal residences still in use. The others are Buckingham Palace in London and the Palace of Holyroodhouse in Edinburgh. The Royal Family traditionally spends Christmas at Windsor Castle.

William the Conqueror built a motte and bailey castle on the chalk cliff overlooking the River Thames. It is unusual because it has two baileys, one on each side of the central motte. The moat was never filled in because the Normans did not know how to raise a sufficient quantity of water.

Henry I was the first sovereign to move into the castle. Henry II built the Round Tower in stone to replace the wooden one. Edward III, who was born in the castle in 1312, transformed it from a garrison and prison to a royal palace.

The heraldic badge of the Royal House of Windsor adopted by King George VI in 1941. It shows the Royal Standard flying from the Round Tower. This is flown when the Queen is in residence. At other times the Union Jack is flown.

c 1070
Norman castle built
1110
Henry I moved into castle
1170
Henry II built Round Tower in stone
1475
St George's Chapel begun
1642
Oliver Cromwell's troops in possession during Civil War
1685
Charles II laid out Long Walk
1824
George IV began reconstruction
1917
British royal family adopted the name of Windsor

The view of Windsor from the river which has changed little since the Round Tower was extended.

Trooping the Colour at Windsor in 1895.

During the Civil War, Windsor Castle was held by the Parliamentarians. Many Royalists were imprisoned there with Charles I, who was executed in 1649. When the monarchy was restored in 1660, Charles II spent the night there before his coronation. He later laid out the three-mile long avenue from the Great Park. George IV had houses demolished to bring the avenue up to the castle walls and added a new gateway. He also had several new towers built and added another storey to the Round Tower, making it twice as high as it was. The workmanship was so good that little alteration has been needed. It gives us the dramatic view we have of the castle from a distance.

Current exhibitions include a display of royal carriages and many of the presents given to the Queen by people all over the world.

Queen Mary's Dolls' House was designed by Sir Edwin Lutyens for Queen Elizabeth II's grandmother in 1921-24. The front of the house can be lifted to show the interior which has everything a royal residence should have, including electricity, lifts and a garage for royal cars.

Tintagel Castle

A map of the mainland and island showing the magician Merlin's cave below the inner ward. According to legend, Merlin found the baby Arthur on the beach.

c AD 700
Pottery evidence of settlement
c 1000
St Juliette's Chapel built
1136-38
Tintagel first mentioned in writings by Geoffrey of Monmouth
1233
Stone castle built
1483
Castle in ruins
1852
Castle repaired and opened to visitors
1933
Excavations begun
1983
Fire uncovers foundations of buildings
1985
Further excavations begun

The ruins of Tintagel Castle stand high above the sea on the coast of north Cornwall. Legend associates it with King Arthur, but no evidence has been found to support this.

It is a natural stronghold, set on an island joined to the mainland by a narrow neck of land. Excavations first suggested that it was a Celtic monastery. This is now thought to be unlikely because early Christian monasteries were not usually abandoned. The pottery found there shows it was inhabited until about AD 700. Most of it came from the Mediterranean and north Africa. It is the largest collection found in Britain and Ireland combined. Tintagel Castle was, perhaps, the stronghold of someone wealthy and powerful. There is no evidence that the castle was occupied again until the 12th century.

The ruins we see today are of the medieval castle built mostly by Richard, Earl of Cornwall and brother of Henry III. The lower and upper wards of the castle on the mainland still stand. The gateway to the inner ward on the island, and the wall surrounding it, were rebuilt in 1852. You can still see the battlements on some of the north wall. You can also see the ruins of the chapel which was built in about 1000, and later enlarged to serve the castle.

In the 14th century, the castle was used as a prison but it was not maintained. It was too expensive because this part of Cornwall was then very isolated. In 1483, the castle was already in ruins and deserted, but the chapel was still in use.

There was a fire on the island in 1983. High winds and rains removed much of the ashy soil. Foundations of small rectangular buildings were revealed. Further excavation is being carried out on these discoveries. It is hoped that this will help solve the mystery of the origin of Tintagel Castle.

An aerial view of the ruins of Tintagel showing inner ward and site of the Great Hall, and the wild Cornish coast.

A pottery wine jar from the eastern Mediterranean.

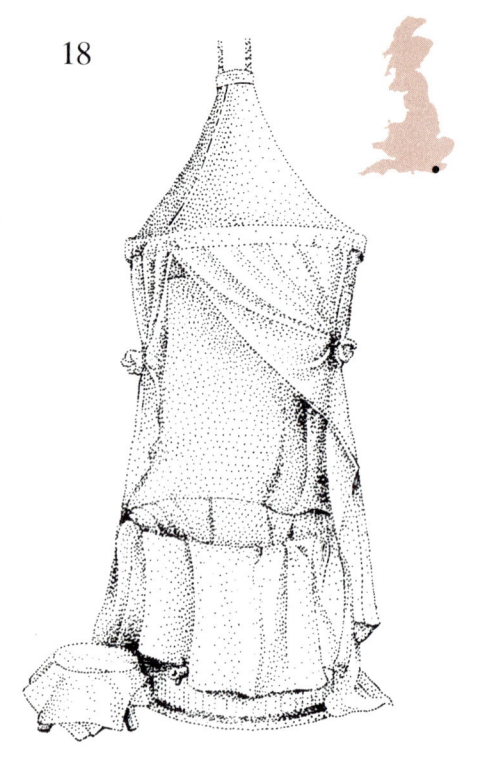

Leeds Castle

A Saxon chief called Led first built a wooden fort on two rocky islands in the River Len in Kent. He chose the site because it was easy to defend. After the Norman conquest in 1066, the manor of Leeds was given to a knight who had fought with William at the Battle of Hastings. His family built the first stone castle. The defences have since been altered. There were inner and outer barbicans, with drawbridges and a moat. The castle keep, called the Gloriette, was built on the smaller island. This was connected by a stone corridor and was the last refuge if the castle was attacked.

In 1278, the castle was given to Queen Eleanor of Castile. Her husband, Edward I, strengthened the defences by adding an outer bailey. This was enclosed by a high wall rising from the water. He added five bastions (towers) and extended the Gate Tower which has a platform (machicolation). Through the holes in the floor, boiling oil and molten lead could be poured onto the enemy below.

For the next 300 years, the castle was owned by queens of England. King Henry VIII made alterations so that it was no longer a fortress but a palace. He built the Maiden's Tower for his maids of honour. By 1552, the castle was no longer a royal palace. It was owned by several families and

A 16th-century bathroom, before stone baths were used. This is a wooden tub draped with a curtain. Linen towels were hung over the sides to protect the queen from the rough surface of the wood. The bath was filled with buckets of water but emptied through the tap at the bottom.

857
Wooden fort built
1119
Stone castle built
1139
First siege of castle
1278
Castle given to Queen Eleanor of Castile
1321
Second siege of castle by Edward II
1552
Castle owned privately
1822
Castle rebuilt
1926
Castle sold to Lady Baillie
1976
Castle opened to public
1981
Visit of Her Majesty the Queen

The Arms of Edward I and Queen Eleanor of Castile on the left and the Arms of the Hon. Lady Baillie on the right. Their flags fly alternately from the masthead on the tower of the Gloriette.

A view of Leeds Castle, built on two islands with the river forming the moat around it.

was also used as a prison. The prisoners set fire to it in 1665 and damaged a great part. The castle was rebuilt in 1822.

In 1926, Lady Baillie bought the castle and had it repaired and refurbished. Visitors can now see how people used to live. In July 1978, the castle's impressive defences were put to a modern day test. Foreign ministers of America, Egypt and Israel met at Leeds Castle for vital Middle East peace talks. The high degree of security needed for such talks showed that Leeds Castle was an ideal setting.

Caernarvon Castle

Caernarvon is situated on the southern end of the Menai Strait in north Wales. The Romans had a fortress in the town in about AD 75-80. Some of the ruins of this can still be seen. The Normans first built a timber motte and bailey castle here. The stone castle was begun on the same site by the English King Edward I as part of a chain of defensive castles in Wales.

It was Edward I who founded the title Prince of Wales. He invested this title on his son, Edward, at Caernarvon Castle in 1301. It became tradition for the reigning monarch to grant this title to the eldest son. The most recent investiture was that of Prince Charles in 1969.

The castle consists of a single defensive area surrounded by a massive curtain wall with towers. The Eagle Tower has walls which are 5.4m (18ft) thick at the base. It once provided accommodation

Castles built in Wales by Edward I included:
1 Beaumaris
2 Conway
3 Caernarvon
4 Harlech
5 Aberystwyth
6 Builth
7 Flint
8 Rhuddlan

1090
Norman timber castle built
1283
Stone castle begun
1301
Prince Edward became first Prince of Wales
1330
Castle finished
1403
Castle besieged by Owain Glyndwr
1538
Castle reported in bad state
1642-48
Castle used as prison
1911
Investiture of Duke of Windsor
1963
Caernarvon made a Royal Borough
1969
Investiture of Prince Charles

A view of Caernarvon Castle showing the majestic castle walls.

on a grand scale. The north wall of the castle now forms part of the town walls of the city of Caernarvon. The castle originally had a moat so it was completely surrounded by water. When the Welsh prince, Owain Glyndwr, attacked the castle in 1403, he was defeated by a force of only 28 men.

Over the next few centuries, the castle fell into disrepair. During the Civil War (1642-48) it was used as a prison and held in turn by Royalists and Parliamentarians. In 1660 Charles II ordered the castle to be demolished, but his orders were not carried out. In the 19th century the town became prosperous again with the slate trade. The castle was in a very bad state and, in 1908, the government stepped in to save it. The interior could not be restored but the huge limestone walls and towers show some of their former glory.

1 The first English Prince of Wales, invested with the title by his father, Edward I, in 1301.

2 A modern investiture. Queen Elizabeth II invested the title on Prince Charles in 1969 in the castle grounds.

Conway Castle

Thomas Telford built the suspension road bridge right up to a tower. This was not originally a gateway but was adapted from an ordinary wall tower and had wall walks added.

1283
Work begun on castle
1290
Besieged by Welsh rebels
1343
Castle reported unsafe
1627
Castle bought by Lord Conway
1642-48
Castle used as garrison during Civil War
1665
Castle abandoned and dismantled
1826
Suspension bridge built
1898
Castle opened to public
1978
Welsh Office responsible for castle

Conway Castle stands on a ledge of rock at the mouth of the River Conway in north Wales. Like Caernarvon and Beaumaris, it could be supplied by sea and was part of Edward I's plan to subdue the Welsh. It was built remarkably quickly from 1283-89.

The castle has eight massive towers and a strong curtain wall with a barbican at each end. The inner ward was the most heavily fortified and contained the king's rooms. The outer ward contained the guard room, kitchens, well and the Great Hall. This was 38m (125ft) long and 12m (38ft) wide. The town walls were built at the same time as the castle to give a strong landward defence. The town walls have twenty-one towers and three double-towered gateways. The castle roofs were made of shingle and slate, which did not stand up to the weather. They were also expensive to replace with lead, and to repair.

The castle fell into disuse and was bought by Lord Conway for only £100 in 1627. During the Civil War it was used by the Royalists but surrendered to the Parliamentarians in 1646. When the monarchy was restored in 1660, the castle was returned to the Conway family. It was beyond repair and the 3rd Lord Conway decided to sell the valuable lead in the roofs and any timber which was not rotten. The main structure of the castle was left abandoned.

The magnificent suspension road bridge was built by Thomas Telford in 1826. The road and the opening of the railway in 1848 brought new prosperity to the town of Conway. There were offers of help to restore the castle and parts of it were opened to the public.

Edward 1 who launched a campaign against the Welsh and built many castles in Wales.

Beaumaris Castle

A view of Beaumaris castle as it would have looked if it had been completed. It shows the outer walls and towers overlooked by the much higher inner walls and towers. The castle dock would have been on the right.

1284
Edward I defeated Welsh. Beau maris (fair marsh) chosen as site for castle
1298
Building stopped for lack of money
1306
Outer wall completed. Building of last four towers began
1609
Castle unusable
1643
Castle used in Civil War
1665
Castle dismantled and lead stripped from roofs
1925
Castle declared an ancient monument

Beaumaris was the last and the largest of the castles built by Edward I in north Wales. It stands on a flat site near the sea on the island of Anglesey. The castle was designed in a series of concentric walls and towers. Work began in 1295.

The first defence was the moat, filled by sea water. If attackers got past this and broke through the outer walls and towers, they would be caught in crossfire from archers in the walls and towers of the inner part of the castle. These were higher than the outer walls so defenders could shoot downwards onto attackers climbing over the outer walls. The outer circle of walls was to have sixteen towers and the inner circle six towers plus two double-towered gatehouses. There were also plans for a castle dock so that sea-going vessels could sail right up to the castle.

Unfortunately, the castle was never finished. At

first 200 quarrymen, 400 stonemasons and 2000 workmen were used. The outer and inner walls were completed but the towers were never built higher than their first storey. The castle we see today is very much as it was left in 1330.

In 1609, the castle was reported as being unusable. Some repairs and restoration were done by 1643. It was used early in the Civil War for the transit of men and materials from Ireland to King Charles I. In 1665, there were reports that parts of the castle were being dismantled. Courtyard buildings and roofs were removed. By the next century the ruins were covered with ivy. In August 1832, however, the inner part of the castle was used for a Royal Eisteddfod (festival) which Princess Victoria, then aged 13, attended. In 1925 the castle was declared an ancient monument. The moat was cleared and the ivy removed.

The castle as it is today viewed from the south. The inner walls and towers were never built above the first storey. The outer ones were never built to their intended height and the gatehouses were not finished.

Edinburgh Castle

The buildings that make up Edinburgh Castle.
1 Esplanade
2 Gatehouse
3 Half Moon Battery
4 The Palace
5 The Scottish National War Memorial
6 St Margaret's Chapel
7 The Governor's House
8 Mill's Mount Battery.

The buildings which make up Edinburgh Castle in Scotland stand on a rock formed by the core of an extinct volcano. It is a natural stronghold. The sides were made steeper by the action of glaciers.

Castle rock was first thought to have been occupied in the 6th century. It became a favourite residence of the Scottish kings. St Margaret died there in 1093 soon after she heard of the deaths of her husband, King Malcolm III and her eldest son. Her youngest son, David I, built a chapel in her memory. St Margaret's Chapel is the oldest part of the castle to survive. Robert the Bruce ordered the destruction of the castle in 1313 so it could not be held by the English. When King David II returned from captivity by the English in 1356, he started rebuilding.

Several kings added to the royal apartments but King James IV started an extensive rebuilding programme during his reign (1488-1513). Mary

The Scottish Crown last used for the coronation of Charles II of Scotland in 1651.

The Edinburgh Tattoo takes place during the Edinburgh Festival on the Esplanade. It is now so popular that elaborate scaffolding is put up to increase the room for the audience.

Queen of Scots gave birth to her son, later James VI of Scotland, in the castle in 1566.

Throughout the centuries of war with the English, the castle was attacked many times. It was constantly rebuilt and fortified. The defences we see today were completed in the 18th century. After the Act of Union in 1707 between Scotland and England, the castle was used mainly as a garrison.

Edinburgh Castle served a similar purpose to the Tower of London. It has been a stronghold, a treasury, a barracks and an arms store, as well as a royal palace. The Scottish Crown Jewels, the crown, sword and sceptre, are stored in the palace. Today the castle is famous for the Edinburgh Tattoo which is held there, and for the one o'clock gun fired every day from Mill's Mount Battery.

11th century
Castle used as royal residence
1093
Death of St Margaret
c 1124
St Margaret's Chapel built
1174-86
Castle held by English garrison
1313
Defences demolished by Scots
1356
Walls built in present form
1544
First record drawing of Edinburgh Castle
1573
Walls blasted to pieces
1650
Castle taken by Oliver Cromwell's troops
1846
St Margaret's Chapel restored
1861
Daily firing of one o'clock gun begun
1947
First Edinburgh Tattoo

Bodiam Castle

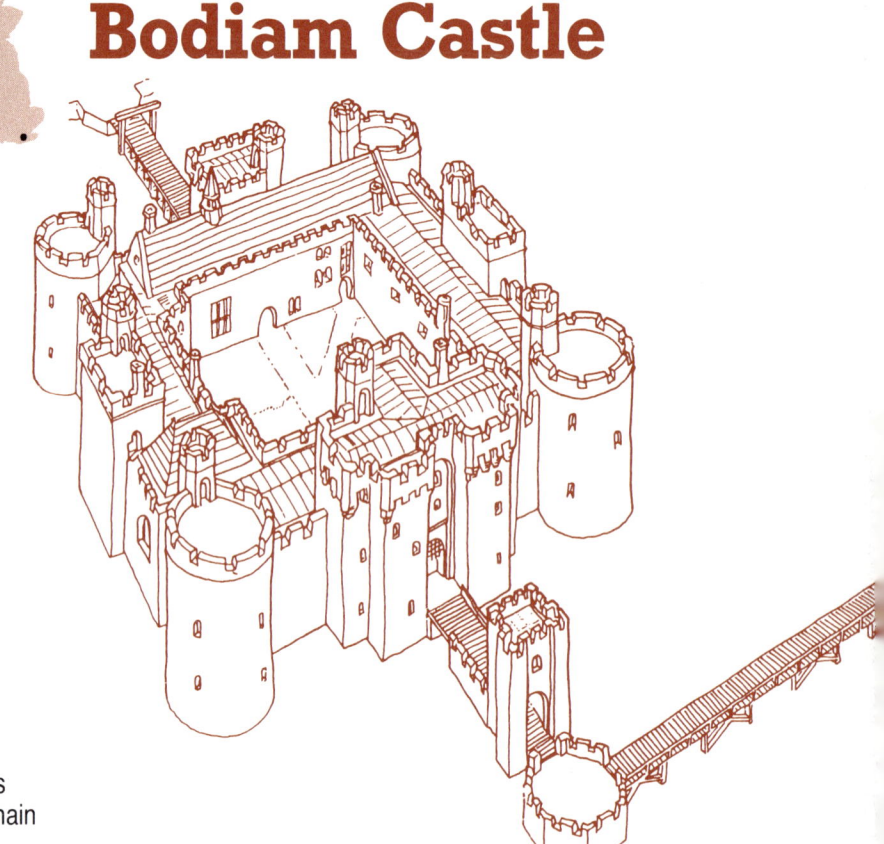

A reconstruction of the north east view of the castle as it would have looked with the wooden bridge at right angles leading to the barbican and main entrance.

1372
English lost control of English Channel
1377
Rye sacked by French
1380
Winchelsea sacked by French
1385
Licence to build castle granted
1388
New castle completed
1483
Castle besieged
1644
Castle captured in Civil War. Interior demolished
1916
Castle sold to Lord Curzon
1925
Castle given to National Trust

Sir Edward Dalyngrigge owned a manor house in Sussex on the River Rother. In 1377 this was a navigable estuary. The French had control of the English Channel and had sacked nearby Rye and Winchelsea. Sir Edward feared that the French would raid his home. He wanted to defend the property and fortify it with battlements. In those days you had to get permission from the king to build a castle. King Richard II gave his permission because Bodiam would be a good defence on the south coast. Sir Edward, however, decided to build a completely new castle instead.

The castle was built to a rectangular plan with towers in each wall and a very wide moat so no one could tunnel under it. Entry to the castle was over a wooden bridge. This was originally built at right angles to the main gate so that defenders could fire on the right sides of the attackers. This

The north view of Bodiam Castle.

was the side unprotected by a shield. After the bridge, there was an island in the middle of the moat with a drawbridge and a barbican, with more drawbridges and portcullises.

By the time the castle was built in 1388, the English were again in control of the channel so the castle was never attacked by the French. It was a private home until the Yorkist King Richard III seized it in 1483 from its Lancastrian owners. During the Civil War (1642-48), the castle was besieged by Parliamentarians who demolished the interior. It was uninhabited for three centuries until Lord Curzon bought it in 1916. He carefully restored and repaired it. When he died in 1925, the castle was given to the National Trust. A large-scale wooden model of the castle as it looked 500 years ago is in the castle museum, together with many relics.

Warwick Castle

Warwick Castle is built on a sandstone cliff overlooking the River Avon, almost in the centre of England. There was a Saxon fortification here, built by Ethelfleda, daughter of Alfred the Great. The site was an obvious one to choose as one side was already protected by the river and cliff. William the Conqueror built a motte and bailey castle there.

A stone castle was built in the 12th century but the castle we see today was almost totally rebuilt in the 14th century. Work was begun by Thomas de Beauchamp, later the 11th Earl of Warwick. His son continued the work until the castle was completed in 1394.

The castle was a fortress as well as a home so defence was very important. If attackers got over the drawbridge to the barbican, they then had to get past an iron portcullis. This led to a narrow passageway with murder holes in the ceiling. Through these defenders could fire at the attackers. At the end there was another portcullis. The outer curtain wall had a walk along which defenders could move freely from tower to tower. Caesar's Tower is almost 45m (147ft) high and has a dungeon and torture chamber. The twelve-sided Guy's Tower is 39m (128ft) high. Each has machicolations. These have gaps in the projecting walls through which heavy stones and quicklime could be thrown onto attackers below.

Visitors can climb up Guy's Tower to get a superb view of the castle grounds and countryside. A former residential wing has been opened to show what life was like in 1898. There are wax statues portraying guests and servants at a royal weekend party.

This represents water in the fantasy in the Conservatory.

916
Saxon fortification built
1068
Norman castle built
1394
Reconstruction of 12th-century stone castle completed
1642-48
Castle used as stronghold during Civil War
1753
Lancelot 'Capability' Brown asked to landscape grounds
1858
Visit of Queen Victoria
1978
Castle sold to Madame Tussaud's
1982
Major repair programme begun
1985
Castle mound opened to visitors

Caesar's Tower with its dungeon. The vaulted chambers above have a display of instruments of torture.

Oliver Cromwell's death mask on display in the Great Hall.

Oliver Cromwell's helmet on view in the Armoury.

Hever Castle

1270
Gatehouse, moat and walls built
1507
Birth of Anne Boleyn
1533
Henry VIII married Anne Boleyn
1536
Anne and her brother beheaded
1538
Castle owned by Henry VIII
1540
Castle given to Anne of Cleves
1557
Death of Anne of Cleves. Castle sold
1903
Castle bought by William Astor. Restoration and building of Tudor style village begun
1963
Castle opened to public
1983
Castle purchased by Broadland Properties Ltd

An aerial view of Hever Castle showing the maze, moat, castle and village. Cellars were built under the village and part of the castle to take the miles of pipes and cables, the water boilers and sewage disposal systems needed for modern plumbing and heating.

The oldest part of Hever Castle on the River Eden in Kent was built as a farmhouse and yard with a protective wall. This was surrounded by a moat with a wooden drawbridge. Two hundred years later, the Bullen or Boleyn family built a Tudor dwelling house within the walls. This was the childhood home of Anne Boleyn. She became Henry VIII's second wife, but was beheaded in 1536. When her father died in 1538, Henry VIII acquired the castle.

The castle was owned by the Crown until Mary Tudor gave it to Sir Edward Waldegrave. He had been Head Warden in the Tower of London when Mary was imprisoned there and this was in return for his kindness to her. There were several owners after this, and it was used by smugglers from the coast. By the end of the 19th century, the castle was occupied by farmers. Ducks and geese swam in the moat, bacon and hams were hung from beams and corn and potatoes stored in chambers. The halls were used as kitchens.

In 1903 William Waldorf Astor, later 1st Viscount Astor of Hever Castle, bought the castle. He restored it and employed craftsmen to make panelling and carved screens. He added bathrooms and central heating. All pipes and wires were carefully concealed. He did not want to spoil the architecture of the original building but he needed to enlarge the property. So he built a village in the Tudor style to provide guest rooms, offices and servants' quarters. The cottages were all connected by corridors. A covered bridge across the moat led to the castle. He also created the lake and gardens with a maze and adventure playground.

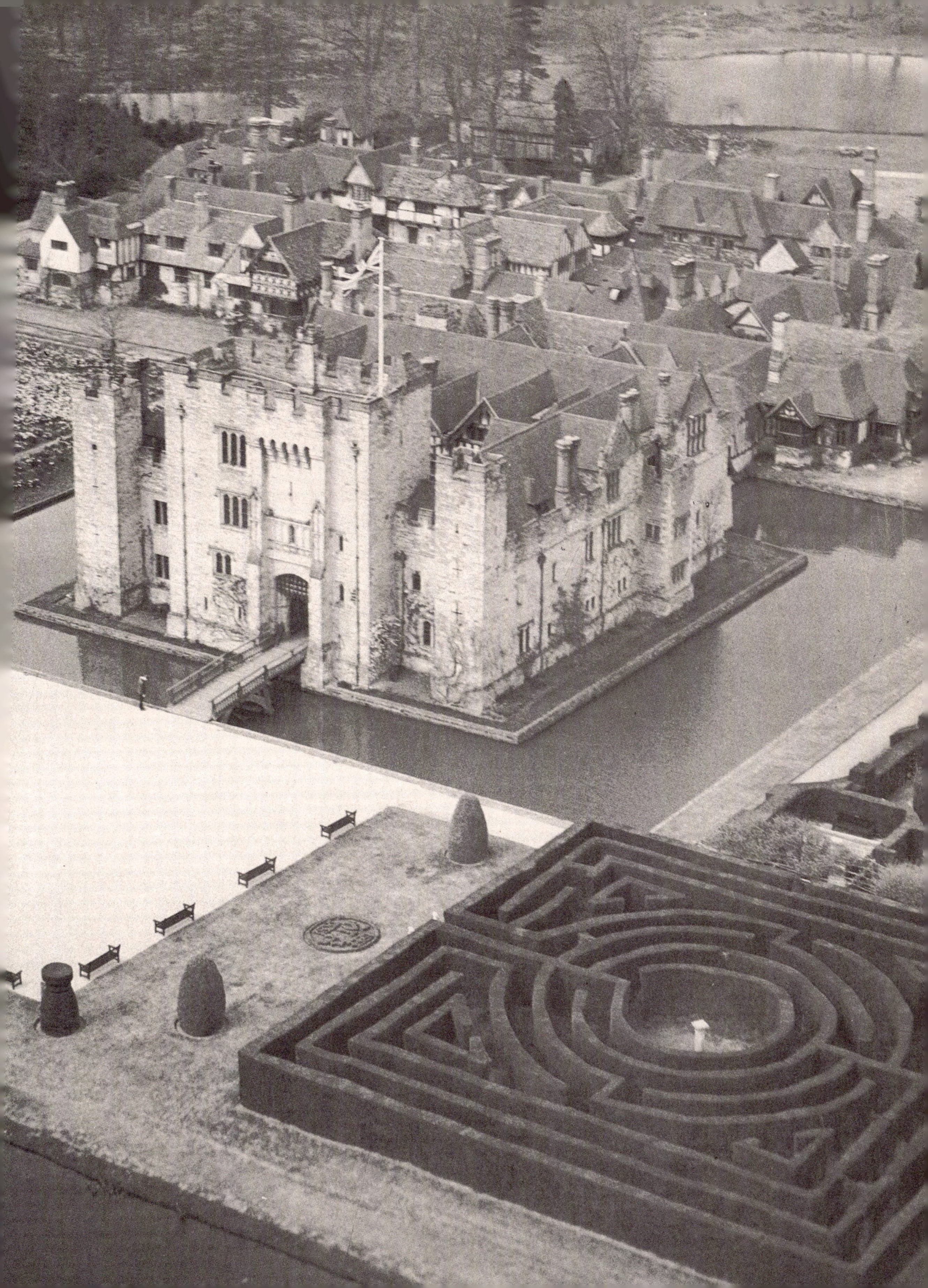

Balmoral Castle

A view of the south front of Balmoral showing the tower with the round turret. The main entrance hall is on the left.

1848
Queen Victoria bought lease on Balmoral
1852
Balmoral purchased
1853
Foundation stone of new castle laid
1855
New castle ready for use
1856
Old house demolished
1861
Prince Albert died at Windsor
1878
Queen Victoria bought Ballochbuie Forest
1901
Queen Victoria died
1925
Main entrance gates installed
1953
Plantation damaged in gale
1983
Pony trekking started

Balmoral Castle in the Grampian Region of Scotland has been a private royal holiday home since 1848. Queen Victoria and Prince Albert bought the property without having seen it. They were delighted with the views of the valley of the River Dee and the place was ideal for shooting, walking, fishing and boating.

They soon found that they needed more space and decided to rebuild Balmoral. They chose a new site a hundred yards away so they could still live in the old house while the new one was being built. It was built of pale grey granite in the Scottish baronial style, and they moved into it in 1855. The towers, turrets and rooms in the connecting wing were not finished until the following year. Then the old castle was demolished and the site marked with a stone.

Prince Albert planned improvements to the grounds and farm buildings. Prince Albert died in 1861 before they were all completed. Queen

Queen Victoria on horseback at Balmoral in 1863, with John Brown, her Highland servant.

Victoria erected a memorial to Prince Albert in the grounds and resolved that everything should continue as he had wished. She herself spent longer periods at Balmoral. When she died in 1901, the property passed to Edward VII and his successors. The royal owners since then have increased the amenities in the castle. It originally had only four bathrooms.

The Royal Family is usually in residence at Balmoral from mid-August to mid-October. The Queen and the Duke of Edinburgh take an interest in the running and improvement of the estate. The Duke of Edinburgh has won driving events with a team of four-in-hand Fell stalking ponies. Visitors can go pony trekking on these ponies and see the Highland cattle, deer and forest reserves which are part of the estate.

The Queen's piper wearing Balmoral tartan. This was designed by Prince Albert in black, red and lavender on a grey background. The tartan and Scots thistle were also used on the interior decor of the castle.

36

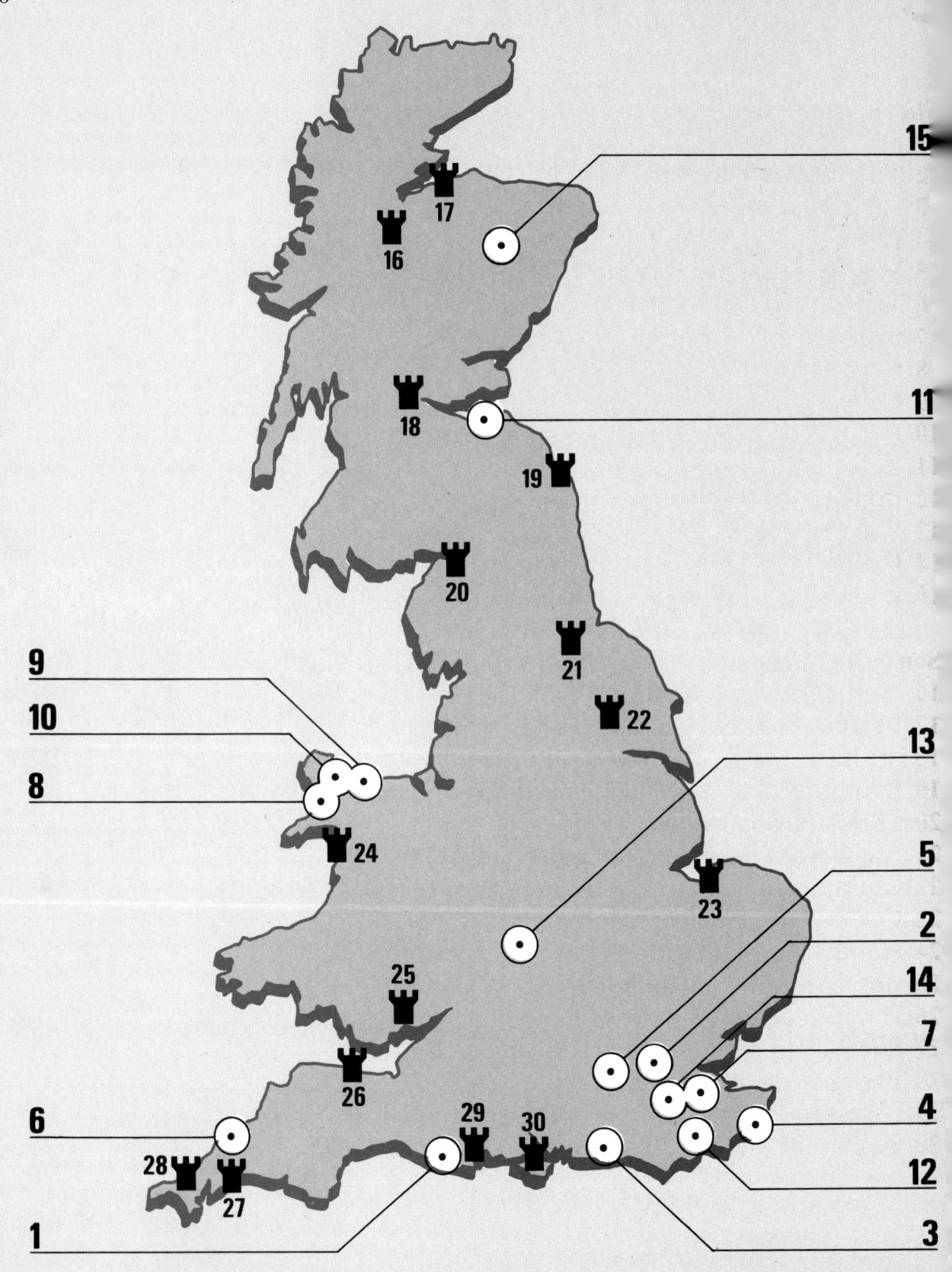

Castles of interest

The castles in this book
1. Maiden Castle, near Dorchester, Dorset
2. The Tower of London, London
3. Arundel Castle, West Sussex
4. Dover Castle, Kent
5. Windsor Castle, Berkshire
6. Tintagel Castle, Cornwall
7. Leeds Castle, Maidstone, Kent
8. Caernarvon Castle, Gwynedd
9. Conway Castle, Gwynedd
10. Beaumaris Castle, Anglesey, Gwynedd
11. Edinburgh Castle, Lothian
12. Bodiam Castle, East Sussex
13. Warwick Castle, Warwickshire
14. Hever Castle, Edenbridge, Kent
15. Balmoral Castle, Grampian

Some other interesting castles
16. Urquhart Castle, Loch Ness, Highlands
17. Cawdor Castle, near Inverness, Highlands
18. Stirling Castle, Central
19. Bamburgh Castle, Northumberland
20. Carlisle Castle, Cumbria
21. Richmond Castle, North Yorkshire
22. Clifford's Tower, York, North Yorkshire
23. Castle Rising, Norfolk
24. Harlech Castle, Gwynedd
25. Cardiff Castle, South Glamorgan
26. Dunster Castle, Somerset
27. St Mawes Castle, Cornwall
28. Pendennis Castle, Cornwall
29. Corfe Castle, Dorset
30. Carisbrooke Castle, Isle of Wight

Things to look for in a castle

1 Coat of arms The heraldic identification of a person or family. All noble families had a coat of arms. It was the only way a knight in armour could be recognised by the coat of arms on his shield.
2 Drawbridge A bridge that can be raised to leave a gap over a moat or ditch to stop the enemy reaching the entrance to a castle.
3 Loopholes Holes in a wall through which weapons could be fired. Usually round, with slits so a defender could see out.
4 Chapel A place of Christian worship, with its own altar, in a larger church or building.
5 Portcullis An iron grating guarding an entrance. It could be raised by chains and let down to stop enemy coming through.
6 Studded door A heavy wooden door with large nails driven into it. It was usually only decorative but looked strong and menacing.
7 Armour A suit, usually chain mail or metal plate, to protect the body from injury during battle. They were often made for horses also.
8 Execution block and axe A wooden block shaped so the head and neck would lie flat making it easier for the executioner to cut the neck with the axe.

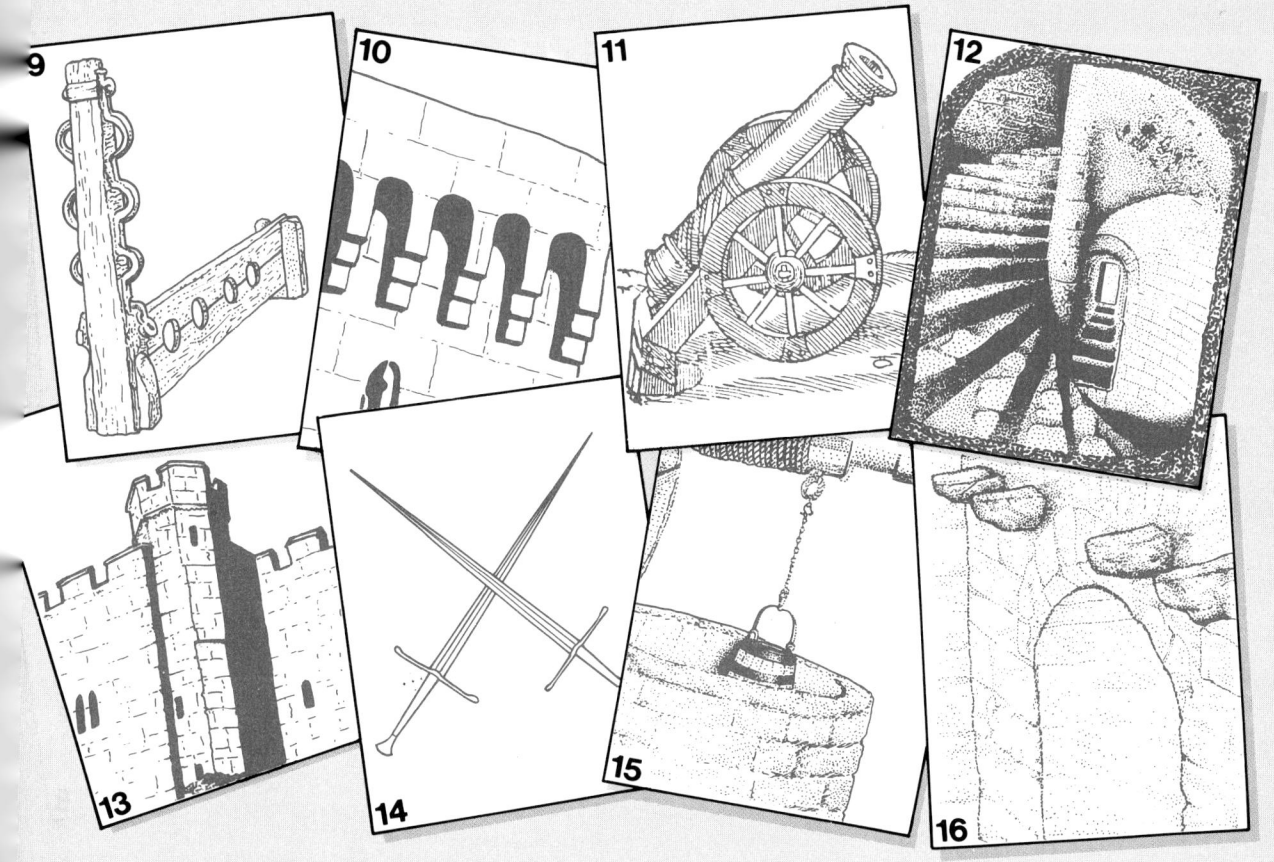

9 Stocks Usually a two-part heavy wooden frame with holes for the head, arms or feet, so victims could be locked up for punishment.
10 Machicolations Openings in the floor of a projecting wall through which missiles could be dropped on enemy below.
11 Cannon A heavy gun with a long metal tube through which balls could be fired. It was mounted on a carriage so it could be moved.
12 Spiral staircase Steps cut into stone and twisted around a single column of stone. Usually very narrow.
13 Crenellations A battlement wall with gaps so defenders could fire weapons through the gaps and shelter behind the solid parts.
14 Trophies Objects like swords and shields captured from the enemy during battle and kept as souvenirs of victories.
15 Well A hole dug into the ground to draw up water from an underground spring or river.
16 Corbels Stone brackets sticking out from a wall to support heavier roof beams.

MANYGATES
MIDDLE SCHOOL
WAKEFIELD

Useful addresses

English Heritage
PO Box 43
Ruislip
Middlesex HA4 0XW
(Historic Buildings and Monuments Commission)
(Written enquiries only)

The National Trust
(for Places of Historic Interest or Natural Beauty)
36 Queen Anne's Gate
London SW1H 9AS
Tel: 01 222 9251

Society for the Protection of Ancient Buildings
37 Spital Square
London E1 6DY
Tel: 01 377 1644

English Tourist Board
4 Grosvenor Gardens
London SW1W 0DJ
Tel: 01 730 3400

Scottish Tourist Board
23 Ravelston Terrace
Edinburgh EH4 3EU
Tel: 031 332 2433

National Trust for Scotland
5 Charlotte Square
Edinburgh EH2 4DU
Tel: 031 226 5922

CADW Welsh Historic Monuments/Wales Tourist Board
Brunel House
2 Fitzalan Road
Cardiff CF2 1UY
Tel: 0222 499909

Northern Ireland Tourist Board
River House
48 High Street
Belfast BT1 2DS
Tel: 0232 231221

Index

Albert, Prince, 34-35
Alfred the Great, 30
Anglesey, 24
Arthur, King, 16
Arundel Castle, 10-11
Astor, William Waldorf (1st Viscount Astor), 32
Badge of the Royal House of Windsor, 14
Baillie, Lady, 18-19
Balmoral Castle, 34-35
Balmoral tartan, 35
Bathroom, 16th century, 19
Beauchamp, Thomas de, 30
Beaumaris Castle, 24-25
Bloody Tower, 8
Bodiam Castle, 28-29
Boleyn, Anne, 9, 32
Boleyn Family, 32
Brown, John, 35
Buckingham Palace, 14
Caernarvon Castle, 20-21
Caesar, Julius, 6
Cannon fire, 13
Charles, Prince, 20, 21
Charles I, King, 15, 25
Charles II
  King, 15, 21
  King of Scotland, 27
Churchill, Sir Winston, 13
Cinque Ports, 12
Civil War, 10, 15, 21, 23, 25, 29
Concentric fortification, 12
Conway, Lord, 23
Conway Castle, 22-23
Cromwell, Oliver 10, 31
Crown Jewels, 8
Curzon, Lord, 29
Dalyngrigge, Sir Edward, 28
David I, King of Scotland, 26
David II, King of Scotland, 26
Dolls' House, Queen Mary's, 15
Dover Castle, 12-13
Edinburgh, Duke of, 35
Edinburgh Castle, 26-27
Edinburgh Tattoo, 27
Edward I, King, 18, 20-21, 22, 24
Edward III, King, 14
Edward V, King, 8
Edward VII, King, 35
Eisteddford, Royal, 25

Eleanor of Castile, 18
Elizabeth, HM the Queen Mother, 13
Elizabeth II, Queen, 21, 35
Ethelfleda, 30
Fitzalan family, 10
Fitzalan-Howard Coat of Arms, 10
George IV, King, 15
Glyndwr, Owain, 21
Henry I, King, 14
Henry II, King, 12, 14
Henry III, King, 8, 13, 17
Henry VIII, King, 9, 18, 32
Hever Castle, 32-33
Holyroodhouse, 14
Howard
  Catherine, 9
  Thomas, 10
Imperial State Crown, 8
James IV, King of Scotland, 27
James VI, King of Scotland, 26
John, King, 12
Julius Caesar, 6
Led, Saxon chief, 18
Leeds Castle, 18-19
Lighthouse, Roman, 12
Lovat, Lord, 8
Maiden Castle, 6-7
Malcolm III, King of Scotland, 26
Margaret, St, 26
Mary, Queen (grandmother of Elizabeth II), 15
Mary I, Queen, (see Tudor, Mary)
Mary Queen of Scots, 11, 26-27
Merlin, 16
Montgomery, Roger de, 10
More, Sir Thomas, 9
Norfolk, Dukes of, 10-11
Northumberland, 8th Earl of, 8
Parts of a castle, 4-5
Percy, Henry, 8
Piper, the Queen's, 35
Prince of Wales, 20, 21
Queen Elizabeth's Pocket Pistol, 12
Ralegh, Sir Walter, 8
Ravens, 9
Richard, Earl of Cornwall, 16
Richard II, King, 28
Richard III, King, 29
Robert the Bruce, 26

Romans, 6-7
Royal Family, 14, 35
Royal Mint, 8
Royal salutes, 9
Royal Treasury, 8
Scottish Crown Jewels, 27
Slingstones, 6-7
Stone Age man, 7
Telford, Thomas, 23
Tintagel Castle, 16-17
Tower Armouries, 9
Tower of London, 8-9
Traitor's Gate, 9
Trooping the Colour, 15
Tudor, Mary, 32
Vespasian, Emperor, 7
Victoria, Queen, 8, 25, 34-35
Waldegrave, Sir Edward, 32
Warwick, 11th Earl of, 30
Warwick Castle, 30-31
White Tower, 8-9
William the Conqueror, 8, 10, 14, 30
Windsor Castle, 14-15
Wine jar, 17
Yeoman Ravenmaster, 9
Yeoman Warders, 9
York, Duke of, 8

41

HOUSES

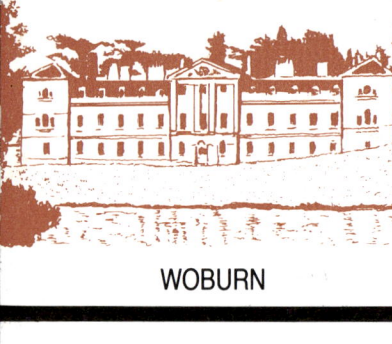

WOBURN	 HAMPTON COURT	 BEAULIEU
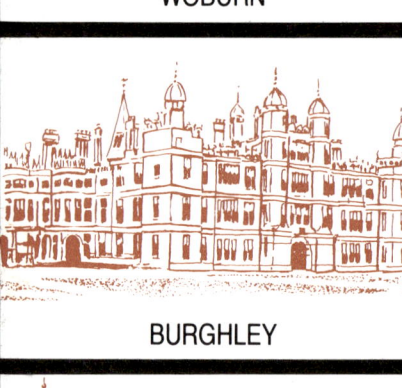 BURGHLEY	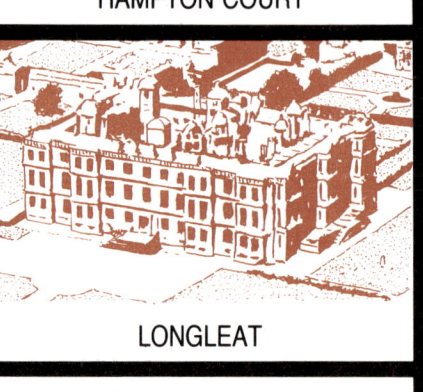 LONGLEAT	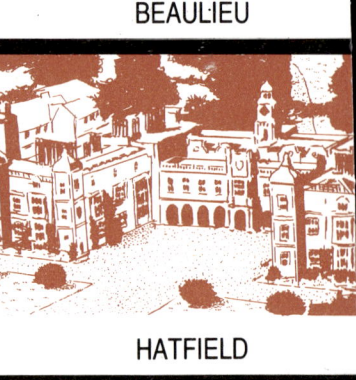 HATFIELD
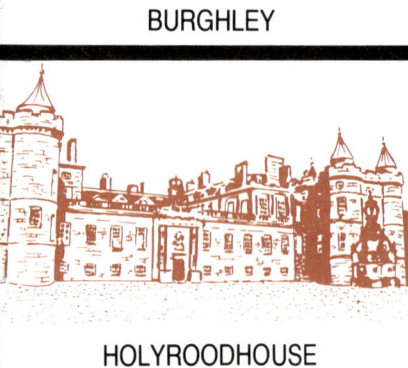 HOLYROODHOUSE	CASTLE HOWARD	BLENHEIM
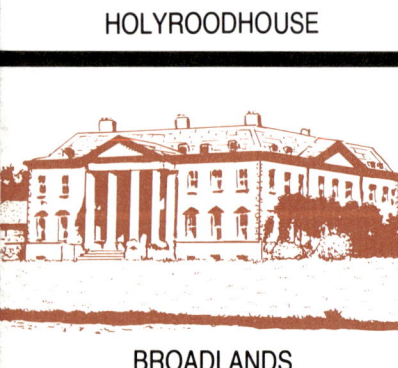 BROADLANDS	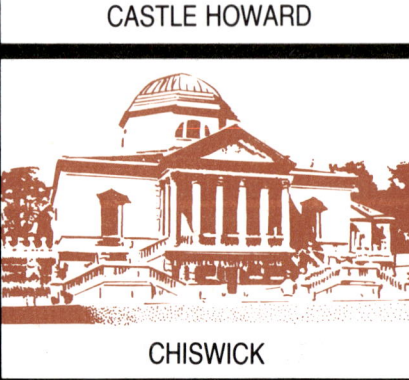 CHISWICK	 10 DOWNING STREET
 HAREWOOD	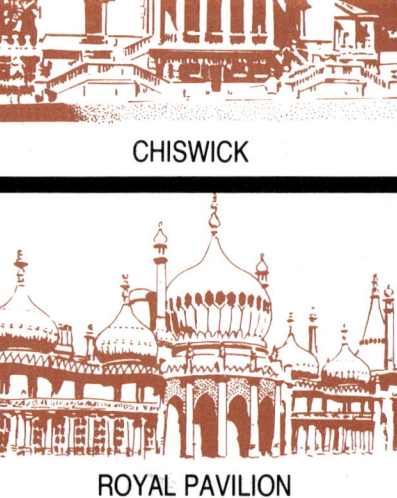 ROYAL PAVILION	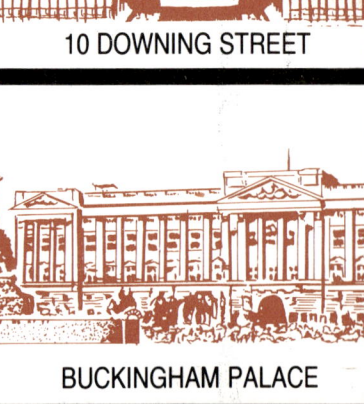 BUCKINGHAM PALACE

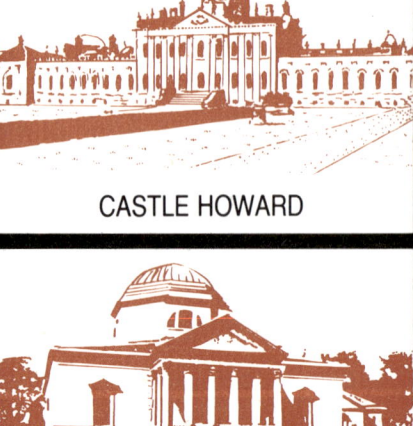